Angels and Economists

Will B. Misquoted

ISBN-13: 978-0-9994189-0-1

Printed in the United States of America

First Printing, 2017

ISBN-13: 978-0-9994189-0-1

Will.B.Misquoted@gmail.com

Table of Contents

Introduction

Economics is the study of the production of goods and services and how they are consumed in a world of scarce resources. Economists observe how people behave to come up with the answers to the questions regarding who, what, why, when, where, and how of the systems surrounding the production and consumption cycles. We economists use this information to advise people on the results that market actions, laws, and policies have on economic matters. However, it is ultimately up to the politicians and citizens to determine what policies they want to pursue to boost both production and consumption. The problem is that economists have usually been ignored, and the facts presented by us bastardized by the people who do not like what the subject of economics has to say on issues regarding wages, welfare, profit, government subsidies, to name a few.

As the study of economic processes highlights awkward truths, it is one of the most depressing subjects a person can study. As a person gains more and more understanding on the subject of economics, they feel increasingly opposed to the policies that on the surface seem noble in intention such as minimum wage, but prove disastrous in results. After a while they become the bad guy on Facebook and other social media platforms who argues against increasing the minimum wage. It all comes to a head when they finally crossover to being the villain who opposes welfare. This can all be blamed on the completely irresponsible move of trying to educate oneself on such a controversial subject. This course of study will inevitably lead those closest to a person to brand them with the scarlet C-Word (Capitalist). From then on, people know them as the person who does not care about the poor.

The downward social spiral a person experiences while communicating ghastly economic ideas and principles is caused by their stubbornness in refusing to go along with socially acceptable economic narratives over economic reality. *It's not smart to argue on principles if your principles lead you to disagree with the majority of your friends and family who want easy answers to explain the factors which lead to wealth and poverty in the world.*

There is a tendency of people who **wish** for a better world to disguise economic opinions (normative economics) as economic facts in an attempt to discredit the science of economics (positive economics). Anytime you hear words like "should" or "deserve", be prepared to hear a narrative and not a fact. If you're smart, you go along with the fantasy and leave the facts for others.

Since there are still people in this world stubborn on living the life of a social outcast and continue their study of economics, I've written this book to provide responses to some of the more common economic fallacies surrounding the questions on poverty a person might encounter from one's friends and families. Economists need to do a better job at educating the public on why we oppose policies such as the minimum wage, welfare, and other policies aimed at *helping the poor*; to truly *help the poor*. My objection to the current policies intended to help the poor is that they aren't well thought out, and as a result they have disastrous consequences on the impoverished. Altruistically everyone wishes to help the poor, but you can't help anybody if you don't honestly address the economic reasons for long-term systemic poverty.

I will focus primarily on the negative effects of economic myths relating to poverty and welfare and how these myths devastate the less fortunate. There are already enough middle class/rich people in the streets arguing against programs and policies aimed at helping the poor on the basis of higher taxes and higher costs of goods and services. This line of arguments just opens the door to an endless rich vs. poor battle and does nothing to definitively address the question of whether or not minimum wage and welfare policies actually help the poor. Though I will briefly acknowledge moral arguments, my goal is to provide clarity on economic subjects by emphasizing cause and effect.

Chapter 1: Minimum Wage

Topic 1: What is Minimum Wage?

The minimum wage is the lowest hourly wage an employer can pay to hire somebody to work for them. In the United States this wage is set by the federal, state, and local governments. Any employer who pays less than the minimum wage breaks the law. The government sets this wage with the intention to help the poorest members of society take home a little bit more money in their paychecks. The federal minimum wage is currently set at $7.25 an hour [1]. Now $7.25 an hour is not a lot of money, but it is better than what some of these people currently earning minimum wage would earn without the law. Now, to a "caring" American this would seem socially, morally, and logically responsible, but reality and fact dictate that minimum wage hurts the poor. To understand why a set minimum wage hurts the poor, we have to first consider the forces that determine how many workers are hired and how the pay of those workers is determined.

You've probably heard before that prices are set by supply and demand. But what does that mean? Basically, prices are set at the point where buyers and sellers agree to trade money for goods and services. From the buyer's point of view, they make purchases when they find a seller that is selling the goods or services they want at a price they can agree on. From the seller's point of view, they sell items when they agree with the amount of money a buyer is offering for the goods or services they have for sale. A trade happens when a buyer and seller find prices they can agree on for a specific good or service. *That is what economists mean when they say that prices and the number of items sold are set by the laws of supply and demand.* Watch an episode of Pawn Stars on the History Channel, and you'll see how prices are set by the buyer and seller in real time. Just as importantly, you will see deals not happening because the buyers and sellers can't reach an agreement on the price.

When people work for a business, the service being sold is labor of the worker, where the worker is the supplier, and the business is the buyer. Just like every other good or service being sold and bought, the society determines the price and quantity traded via supply and demand. The worker lets the business know how much money they need the business to pay them in order for them to supply the business with labor. Reciprocally, the business lets the worker know how much they're willing to pay the worker for their labor. If they can come to a deal, just like our Pawn Stars example above, then the worker gets paid by the employer, and the business gets labor from the worker in return. If they cannot come to an agreement, the worker stays unemployed, and the business gets no labor from the worker.

Now that we have briefly explained supply and demand, we can talk about how minimum wages impact the supply and demand of workers and to do that I'll introduce another economic concept known as "**Price Floors**". A price floor is the lowest price which you can legally sell an item. For example, if the government were to impose a $5 price floor on a gallon of gas, it would make it illegal to sell a gallon of gas for any less than $5. If the buyer and seller of gasoline agree that $2.50 is the best price for gas, they still are legally bound to sell the gas for $5 or more.

The problem with price floors is they interfere with the decision of buyers and sellers to determine the prices and quantities they are willing to buy and supply for goods and services. This normally causes fewer goods and services from being sold because all the prices of price floor controlled goods are higher than that the consumer would buy them at. Even if the supplier is willing to supply the buyer with goods at prices lower than the minimum price the government sets, they are unable to do it because selling at prices below the price floor is illegal. Going back to our gasoline example, if buyers and sellers agree to trade at a price of $2.50 for a gallon of gas, but a price floor of $5 per gallon is put in place by the government, than fewer gallons of gas

8

would be sold. This is simply because there would be fewer buyers willing to pay $5.00 a gallon than $2.50 for a gallon of gas.

The minimum wage is the most well-known example of a price floor. My friend and I both might be willing to work for $5 an hour to sell jeans at Abercrombie (other perks of the job include getting hit on by attractive women), and Abercrombie might be willing to give us jobs at $10 an hour total for the both of us, but because there is a minimum wage in place Abercrombie has to pay us both at least $7.25 an hour or else it will be illegal to hire us. In that scenario, only one of us is going to get the job. Therefore, this is the problem with minimum wage—it doesn't let the buyer and seller decide at what prices they can make a deal when it comes to the sale and purchase of labor.

Imagine it's the end of the winter season, and a store is left with a lot of unsold winter gear. What do they do? Most people who have worked in retail or is a savvy shopper should know the answer to this. To clear inventory and generate revenue, the store will announce a sale and sell their products at discounted rates, which will clear out their inventory and put some cash in their pocket. It's an unchanging law of economics that if a good or service is offered for sale at a lower price, it will sell much quicker than if the price was higher.

Similarly, what does one do if they find themselves unemployed and having a tough time finding a job? Skilled workers lower the amount of money they're willing to accept for their next job, in order to land a job as soon as possible. The minimum wage removes the ability of unskilled or low-skilled workers from doing the same. Unskilled or lower skilled workers are unable to say to an employer, "I will work for $5.00 an hour if you'll hire me today." The minimum wage commands at least $7.25 an hour, eliminating their ability to bargain down to secure a job. Without the ability to negotiate earnings below the set minimum wage, people with no/low skills have a much tougher time finding the first job; ultimately removing opportunities to work and accumulate skills early on.

Topic 2: Why can some people only earn minimum wage?

You would probably agree that the vast majority of those earning minimum wage have low or no job skills. When I was a teenager, the highest paying job I could have found would probably be below the minimum wage, because I had no skills. Like most Americans today, I earn more than the minimum wage. What changed between the teenage me and the present me (besides the beer gut)? I acquired skills both on the job and through education. These new skills increased the amount of money that employers are willing to pay me, because I can do more for them with the skills I acquired. Let's explore the way in which supply and demand sets the prices of workers at different levels of skill.

*Supply and Demand Reasons for why Inexperienced Workers Make
Less Money than Skilled Workers:*

Supply:

Inexperienced workers tend to start out in jobs with
skillsets that can be taught in a very short time to just about
anyone. This explains the high concentration of minimum wage
retail and fast food workers (I've worked in both). In these jobs
workers usually perform a variety of very simple tasks that are
typically mastered very quickly.

Since most people can be taught the job, there is a high
supply of potential candidates who can perform minimum wage
level work. Essentially, any able-bodied person can do it, as
opposed to high-skilled jobs that demand experience and training
to perform specialized tasks. For example, most employees within
my office building could roll up their sleeves and, with less than a
day's worth of training, be taught to work in the various functions
of a retail or fast food environment. Whereas it would be near

impossible to find fast food workers in the country, that could replace all the accountants and financial analysts in my company without years of training and education. This is not to suggest that high-skilled workers are naturally better or smarter than the inexperienced workers; in the scenario presented above, the matter of obtaining the skills to perform accounting functions requires more time and experience. High-skilled workers acquire expertise in their fields over many years. What is normally forgotten in the discussion is that the vast majority of skilled workers worked "grunt jobs" at one point or another in their careers. This is a fact normally dismissed by those who choose not to hear it.

Many more workers apply for a single minimum wage job opening as opposed to a high-skilled job opening, and most of these potential workers are willing to accept a lower pay to land a job as they possess very few job skills. After a business hires a fast food worker and when the time to negotiate the wage comes, the business doesn't have to offer much to the new hire. If the new hire doesn't accept the wage, the business can call a multitude of other people who applied before to fill that spot. This high supply of inexperienced workers is the number one supply based reason why the wages for inexperienced workers are low.

Demand:

Demand for labor is derived from the value that employers receive from employing workers. An employer will always hire workers as long as they believe that they will receive more money from the employees' labor than it costs to employ them. Let's run through another quick scenario to highlight this concept.

If we raise the minimum wage to, let's say, $15 an hour, and I as an employer only receive $14 of benefit from one of my employees, the employee would have to hit the streets because the employee literally is costing me more money to employ than their labor is worth to me as an employer.

Facts show that unskilled or low-skilled workers don't contribute much in benefit for employers in their individual roles (again, not a moral judgment, just a business one). Let's go back to our fast food example, if there is only one cashier at a burger joint and that burger joint makes $200 an hour by selling burgers, how much value does that cashier add per hour to the business? I asked that question a lot to people on the street, and most people answer $200 an hour. Well that's simply not true. What those answering the question failed to take into account is all the other inputs leading that business to sell their burgers.

The cashier did not cook and package the finished burgers, nor did they drive the beef patty to the store. They didn't slaughter the cow to make the beef patty, and they didn't raise or feed the cow. The same logic applies for all the other ingredients that went into the making the burger (lettuce, pickles, tomatoes, etc.). Finally, you also have to add in the cost of building and maintaining the restaurant. If were to list all the people who had a hand in allowing the customer to purchase that burger, it would be as long as the credits at the end of a movie. Returning to the cashier's contribution, they ring up orders and hand the customers their food. It is obviously a very low value function (I'm picking only on the cashiers at fast food restaurants because I was one for quite long).

Why do inexperienced, low skilled workers earn low pay? There is a high supply of people willing and able to do their jobs, and low skilled workers don't add much value to the business they work for with the function they perform. That statement might sound harsh and insensitive to some, but economic truth is normally ugly.

Topic 3: Won't raising the minimum wage help the poor?

No, raising the minimum wage is absolutely not going to help the poor. The paramount reason being employers will have to exercise options for cutting labor costs, if the price of labor is raised. Employers could minimize staff, cut hours, or automate tasks. Most employers will do all the above-mentioned things if the minimum wage is set above the wage they're willing to pay for their employees. Why? They have limited resources with which to produce. If they don't cut costs, they'll be unable to produce products at a price their customers are willing to purchase.

Labor is like any other good or service that people purchase in their daily life. It is affected by supply and demand. If a business charges more for hamburgers, you will purchase fewer hamburgers. If your supermarket charges more for beer, the parties you attend will be BYOB because the person throwing them will purchase less beer. We will purchase less when items cost more. Naturally a business will purchase less labor when that cost increases. It is because a business has limited resources just like every one of us. If they are wrong for buying less labor when the government makes it more expensive for them to purchase it, then we as consumers are wrong for buying less beers and hamburgers when the store down the street charges you more money for those artery clogging burgers and fine craft brews.

Consequently, minimum wages also cause businesses to raise their prices (up to a price that consumers are willing to pay, before they stop consuming) to cover the increased costs of employing inexperienced workers. With higher minimum wages, it will cost a bit more to eat out, buy groceries, send kids to daycare, etc. When the minimum wage increases, people with limited skills struggle to find a job, everything they purchase will be a bit more expensive. As a response to having fewer customers, businesses will trim down on their workforce. By now you may understand that the concept and implementation of minimum wage decimates the poor, but how does an increased minimum wage impact the wealthy?

Simply put a minimum wage doesn't distress the wealthy. When the government mandates a minimum wage increase, the income of the wealthy remains unchanged. Because affluent workers don't earn minimum wage, their jobs are largely unaffected. When the grocery store prices increases to cover the costs of the minimum wage workers, rich folks won't have to decrease consumption as much as the poor person because they are better equipped to afford the increase. The people in a society who are most affected negatively by the minimum wage law is, of course, the poor.

Topic 4: What is the evidence that the minimum wage really causes unemployment? Why doesn't the unemployment rate rise very much when the wage is raised?

Elementary school math has the answer to the question of why the unemployment rate doesn't go up very much when the minimum wage is raised. There aren't that many people who work for minimum wage—only 3.9% of American workers according to the Bureau of Labor Statistics [1]. The rest of the working population earns more than the minimum wage. Using that information, we can deduce that *if every single worker making minimum wage lost their job due to a minimum wage hike, the unemployment rate would only rise by 3.9%.*

Doing some simple math, let's say a minimum wage increase of $2 an hour causes the unemployment among those currently earning minimum wage to rise by 20% (completely hypothetical) which would be disastrous to low skilled workers. But if we calculate the *overall* unemployment rate (the statistic normally reported by mainstream media outlets), the rate would only increase by a whopping .78%! (That's right simple elementary math - 100% x 3.9% x 20% = 0.78%). You will not read or hear any breaking news stories on the unemployment rate increasing less than 1%, but you've just taken 20% of jobs away from those at the bottom. The key to tracking the harm caused by the minimum wage on the poor, is to calculate the unemployment numbers for only those that have no/low skills, since these are the groups most likely to be earning minimum wage.

Teenagers are groups that economists would consider low skilled. It is very unlikely they have been working long enough to have accumulated job skills. Analyzing unemployment among teenagers, we see increasing rates for this group after minimum wages are raised [10]. Unfortunately, the only people who tend to track and discuss the specific unemployment demographics among these employers are old and boring economists like me.

Long term data show that the minimum wage law expands the number of people in the category of no/low skills. Although only 3.9% of workers work for the minimum wage at any given time, the majority of those starting out in the work force (young workers) needed those minimum wage jobs to start developing job skills that lead to higher paying jobs down the road [1], including me.

Unemployment rates are also skewed by the methods that count who is unemployed. The rate is not based on the number of Americans who are out of work. It is calculated by the number of Americans out of work and actively looking for a job within the past 4 weeks. Those without a job AND not seeking work are neither "employed" nor "unemployed"; they are quietly swept under the rug and considered out of the labor force [2]. Let's use this information to explore why the unemployment rate is not a great metric to measure the job losses in low skilled workers when a minimum wage is present.

So how and where do low-skilled workers fit into this concept and calculation of unemployment? No/low skilled workers are usually young with fewer financial obligations and or requirements. They're probably not looking for jobs as if their next meal depended on it. Anecdotally, most teenagers are insecure, and they tend to avoid rejection like the plague. So, it really only takes a few rejections to get them to stop applying for jobs. Therefore, most of this entire group goes uncounted as officially unemployed.

In high school my friends and I would periodically complete job applications at various companies. We were usually turned down, because we had no experience, and offered no real skill or benefits to the business. Moreover, the employer would be forced to pay us minimum wage if they did hire us. Rejections from these employers often led to discouragement and eliminated our desire to actively seek work. If you go recall how unemployment is calculated, we were by our own definitions, unemployed. However, since we had not put out applications in the prior 4 weeks, most of us would not be reported in the "official unemployment numbers."

The two reasons that the *overall* unemployment rate doesn't rise much when minimum wages are hiked is due to the fact that: Minimum Wages don't affect most of the working population; and a portion of the no/low skilled workers that lose out on job opportunities are not counted, due to the way the official Unemployment Rate is calculated. The reason we do know that job losses occur due to the minimum wage is that the unemployment rate in specific groups we would expect to be no/low skilled, rise when the wage is raised.

Topic 5: How is somebody supposed to live off of the minimum wage?

       I earned minimum wage once, and I'm willing to bet that more than half of you reading this book earned it as well during some point in your working life. The majority of us former and current minimum wage workers are still alive and kicking. Most however, seem to forget that this period of earning minimum wage only covers a short span of time in the careers of most workers. That's why only 3.9% of people earn it at a given time, but the bulk of able-bodied American's have made the minimum wage or less, sometime in their life. This nostalgic exercise serves (not to remind you of the awful burger flipping or table waiting) to demonstrate how quickly people enter the workforce earning minimum wage, and then transition into earning higher pay as they gain more skills. Otherwise, the percentage of workers making minimum wage would be much higher than 3.9%.

Typically, what I have seen with people in my own life is a transition to a higher paying role as early as six months to a year after starting a minimum wage job. For those wondering how to survive during those low wage times, the following help most do it:

1. Family - This is probably the number one place most people get help while starting out at a minimum wage job. Family usually offers food, shelter, and additional support, if they can. For me, family is where I obtained financial support when I earned minimum wage while working at a grocery store stocking shelves. Not everybody has this option, so we have to talk about alternatives to family.

2. Friends - This is typically the second place people go for help

during their minimum wage job. Regularly, this comes in the form of a place to crash or a few roommates to help pay rent. Friends also prove a valuable source to learn which companies are hiring people their age and experience level, in addition to understanding what skills to pursue for that higher paying job. Not everybody has this option either.

3. Charity – These are generally non-profit entities that offer free hot meals, shelter, groceries, clinics, career advisement centers, day care, and housing, to name a few. Charity will almost always have enough resources to care for the truly needy. I've volunteered at many different organizations over the years. In my experience, I can assure you that everyone willing to accept charity for assistance receives the help they need to survive. I have seen outrageously long lines at food kitchens before. Despite the long wait, everyone leaves with food in their stomachs.

4. Community - This is an oft-forgotten area that low-skilled workers should go for help. The difference between charity and the community, is that the community is not organized, and is usually just people you encounter in your daily life. If you are that person struggling on minimum wage, or know someone who is, there are always citizens in your own community who will offer great advice on how to obtain the resources needed to survive during the hardship, and what you need to do to be successful. Just put yourself out there and ask for help. You would be amazed at the number of people willing to assist you with job information and material resources. I have personally given out locations of shelters and food kitchens to people who appeared to need help. I've also directed a few struggling grads to employment opportunities at companies I've worked for in the past.

Topic 6: Wouldn't a higher minimum wage improve the economy since minimum wage workers will have more money to spend on goods and services?

I've shown that minimum wage earners would have less money overall, as there would be less opportunities available for them to work. However, let's assume that a minimum wage law passes simultaneously with a law that employers must hire workers at their current pace (this is a complete fantasy). Does more money going to the minimum wage workers actually provide them with greater purchasing power? The economists' answer is a resounding no.

The major problem in this scenario is that there will be significantly decreased production of goods and services. If all the government had to do was GIVE everyone more money to sustain a higher standard of living, they would just replace $1 bills with

$1,000 bills and simply throw money out of planes. The problem is we don't go to work to earn money just to stare at paper bills. We go to work so that money we earn, can be used to purchase the goods and services we want. Money is just the medium that we use to make trade easier and not the actual end product that we consume. We use money for trade, because it's easier to carry around paper bills in your pocket, as opposed to carrying around widgets to trade. The reason why consumers have limited goods and services to consume is because we live in a world of scarce resources, and it takes a lot of "behind-the-scenes" work to get any product to market.

If government mandates that businesses raise their wages without any power to lay off workers (ignoring the fact in the real world, they would just close up shop), they will have to take the resources they're going to use to pay their workers from the company's capital purchases (equipment used to produce goods and services). As a result, no matter how many more workers they hire and how hard those workers work, they will be producing less goods and services. That's because businesses will be spending more money on labor and less on capital (i.e. factory equipment, trucks, construction equipment, buildings, office supplies, to name a few.). Additionally, existing capital that businesses already own are constantly breaking down, and in need of repair or replacement. Increased payments going to labor will translate to less money invested into the expansion and maintenance of existing capital. Try cooking dinner tonight without your stove, oven, or microwave, and you'll fully appreciate why capital is just as important as labor when it comes to producing any product. Despite having three times the number of hands in the kitchen helping with preparation, without the convenience of modern kitchen appliances, dinner will take a longer time to prepare.

In a scenario where higher minimum wages are imposed without fear of layoffs, everyone in our society would earn more money, but there would be fewer goods and services produced. More resources will be used for short-term consumption as most would have more money in their pockets, fewer resources will be spent to replenish and expand capital as businesses will have less money to spend on machinery. The result is prices go up, as more dollars in circulation decreases the value of the *overall* dollar, and fewer goods to go around increases the price of the goods for sale. This is what is known in economics as **inflation**.

There is one, and only one, way to increase the standard of living for everyone in society. What is that *one way*? Increase the production of goods and services. This requires a system that balances both wages and capital investment. Artificially tweaking either will lead to market distortions which decrease production and consumption. This is exactly what results when we try to manipulate wages via minimum wage.

Topic 7: Wouldn't employers just pay employees pennies for their labor, if there were no minimum wage enforced by the government?

An employer might want to pay someone less, but their greed is checked by the same system as ours—supply and demand. For example, I might want to buy a boat for $1, but no one in their right mind will sell me a new (or even slightly used) boat at that price. In perpetual futility I could try to recruit homeless people for landscaping work at $1 a day wages and I guarantee that I'd hire no one!

Similarly for employers; they might want to pay very little for labor, but nobody will work without getting something in return. Some critics of this point to unpaid interns as an example of free labor; however they neglect to mention the amazing skills they receive from internships, which increases their future potential earnings. Let's not forget about all the people that owe their fame and fortune directly to the skills and experience they gained from their internship (Monica Lewinsky comes to mind).

Let's explore this question of how wages are set from a different angle. If the minimum wage law is the one regulation stopping employers from paying employee's very little to work for them, then why do only 3.9% of American workers earn minimum wage?

I earn more than minimum wage. Why is my employer paying more than they legally have to? Why are employers all over America paying 96.1% of working Americans more money than they are legally bound to? America is a free market. In this free market system, employers must compete for my labor. I can't force employers to hire me if I make outrageous demands (unless my skills are extraordinarily rare and valuable), and they can't force me to work for them, so I'm empowered to choose the terms I'm willing to accept for my labor. Conversely, employers can also decide these same terms. The beauty of this system is that if either side disagrees with the demands of the other, the deal never happens. This system maintain sensibility of both parties when negotiating employment.

In an utterly ridiculous scenario, if I walked into work on a Monday morning and my boss explains that they have to lower my salary to the minimum wage, what would happen? Apart from a customary cursing, I'd send out my resume to companies that will offer market prices for my labor, based on the skills I have accumulated in my working career. My employer has no method to retain me if they offer a wage I know is too low for the skills I have gained through my employment history and education. This is NOT an entitlement. Like every other worker the skills I have acquired while suffering through the drudgery of work and school, has a certain value to employers. Workers are able to quickly determine what their skills are worth in the labor market by looking at the offers other employers are making to the workers with similar skills. Luckily in our expanding digital world, we can do this with a few swift clicks of the mouse.

If every employer in the country were to meet, and somehow force government to abolish the minimum wage, then went further collectively agreeing to not pay any employees more than $1 an hour for their labor, they still couldn't obtain labor at this rate. Why? No one will work for any employer for $1 a day, unless they get compensated in other ways. There is zero incentive to acquire skills in this absurd scheme. People would naturally quit their jobs, sleep in, and spend time with their families. They would probably barter and trade amongst themselves to acquire the goods and services they need to survive. For those businesses resolute on paying $1 an hour, they'll go bankrupt without any workers tending to their operations.

Sales jobs are the perfect example of people working with the promise of hefty paychecks, then leaving when they aren't appropriately compensated. Many jobs in sales are based in commission (i.e. you earn a percentage of what you sell). In simplest terms, if you don't make any sales, you don't get paid. During the recruiting phase, sales managers often give the promise of easy sales and huge commissions. Unfortunately, most people suck at sales (myself included), and many of them, upon realizing this, will quickly abandon ship once they aren't able to secure commissions. Try as the employers might to convince their employees to stay, crappy sales agents all leave the industry within the first few pay periods when they can't earn a wage.

The only way to break the laws of supply and demand in the case of setting wages is via force. If businesses at large were determined to use governments to legislate an effective way for employers to acquire cheap labor, it would be to legalize kidnapping in order to bring workers to factories or offices. This would also require the lawful use of violence to extract labor from them. In a nutshell, slavery would need to be legalized to effectively control wages.

With every good or service purchase, regardless whether it's a boat or labor, the unshakeable law of economics remains the same—Supply and Demand will determine the price. A high supply of workers and low demand for a particular skillset will result in lower pay for low-skilled workers. Whereas a low supply of high-skilled workers and a high demand for their labor will generate higher wages. The key to getting a higher pay for your labor is getting specialized skills that employers will pay for. The best way to do that is to accumulate skills while working.

Topic 8: Why does Costco pay their employees more money than Walmart for the same work?

I listen to many people ask this question when talking about whether or not employers should pay their employees more. Unscientifically, I hear the argument "Costco pays their employees much more than Walmart and offers their employees benefits too." While that's awesome for Costco employees, and I certainly applaud Costco for doing it, Costco is able to afford higher pay, because they operate entirely differently from Walmart.

The following are three examples of how Costco operates differently from Walmart:

1. *Costco charges money for the privilege to shop at their stores.* In the United States, Costco charges a $55 annual

membership fee for their cheapest level of membership (Gold Star) As of February 15, 2015, Costco had 44.6 million paid cardholders [3]. If you do the math on this, it's a multibillion-dollar stream of revenue they receive simply for allowing consumers to shop at their stores. Walmart stores don't charge a membership fee and, therefore, don't receive the same multibillion-dollar revenue from memberships.

2. *Costco sells items in bulk.* This allows Costco's customers to save money, and further allows Costco suppliers to charge less on the goods they sell. For most businesses it will usually cost less per unit to produce and sell at higher quantities than selling smaller amounts of a particular good. Economists call this bulk savings "Economies of Scale". In our own lives we most often see the concept of Economies of Scale at work when we cook in bulk. It takes less time and electricity for us to cook a large pot of spaghetti and

meatballs that fill four bowls, than to cook the same quantity separately. If you calculate the savings on a multimillion-unit scale, you begin to see the massive savings Costco is generating by selling items in bulk.

3. Costco is able to use a warehouse-style store layout to sell goods, because they are selling goods in bulk. For most items, Costco doesn't stock the shelves. They load up a pallet and move that to the area where the goods will be sold. Then they simply replace the pallet with another one when those items are running low. Whereas Walmart has to not only load up the skid, but also employ workers to stock the shelves. Costco is able to greatly reduce the amount of labor involved with replenishing their merchandise on the sales floor because of this.

Let's see what would happen if we force Walmart and other retailers to adopt the exact Costco model in an effort, to pay

Walmart workers more. I counted the number of stores I went to this week, and it was around 15 (Walmart, Target, Home Depot, various clothing retailers, among others). I would have had to pay membership fees at every single one of those stores to mimic Costco's business model. Doing this would add another $825 (15 * 55 = $825) out of my wallet every year just to have the privilege of purchasing items from the stores I went to this week alone. If I factor in the other stores I go to throughout the year, I'd probably be paying thousands of dollars in membership fees alone! Additionally if every business adopted the Costco model, we would be required to buy everything in bulk. Instead of popping into the grocery store to buy a single Greek yogurt after my workout, I would have to buy a pack of 18!

Those who argue that Walmart and similar retailers should pay as much as Costco, are singling out one desirable aspect of how Costco operates (higher pay for workers), and completely disregarding the complex differences in how these businesses achieve operational goals. From a supply and demand perspective, the Costco business model increases its demand for labor because it earns higher profit from its operations. And due to the vast differences in how the two stores operate, it's evident to those who have worked in retail that Costco's business requires more skills than Walmart's business (i.e. ability to use a cherry picker, direct sales skills, to name a few).

Even with these different business models, it makes everyone richer that both Costco and Walmart both exist. Both of the stores allow consumers to save money on different goods and services. I can buy a two-year supply of batteries and other goods I need to purchase in bulk with sales at Costco. While also saving tons on my weekly grocery bill at Walmart for those items I don't want to purchase in bulk. Moreover, Walmart has a greater variety of brands than Costco. Through their business operations, both businesses employ thousands of people from low-skilled workers in their retail operations to better-paid truck drivers, warehouse workers, procurement teams, back office workers, among others.

Topic 9: CEOs of large corporations earn millions of dollars a year. Why can't we just take the money and resources from highly paid workers to pay minimum wage workers more?

I hear this question from those upset about the wages of low-skilled or unskilled workers. For a long time I shared their outrage. It just doesn't seem fair that some people can have so much, while others have so little. But the law of supply and demand reigns sovereign over this issue as well. I will not justify or discuss the morality of the high pay that executives receive; I will simply explain how and why their pay is so high.

Pay of top-level executives is determined by supply and demand like the rest of the workers in a society. The demand side reason for the amount of money a board of directors is willing to pay is determined by the perceived benefit that a new hire offers the company. The supply-side reason is determined by the number of suitable candidates available to them.

In regards to the demand for executives, company shareholders must decide what traits they require to fill positions (education, experience, skills, among others). On the supply-side, companies must evaluate the quantity of eligible candidates that best fit the description of the skills and experience required for the job. The dominant supply and demand reason for why executives earn so much money is because the supply of the candidates who meet rigorous company leadership standards is often times very low; because they are demanding extraordinary resumes to fill these high positions. The result is vigorous competition among different companies to hire the same people, ultimately leading to higher prices for executives.

If companies offer too little money, nobody with the required experience is going to be willing to take the job offered. Candidates can earn more money at other companies based off of their skills, experience, and the education they have. This is the same reason why I don't quit my job and go work at the burger joint down the street. The available alternatives to me will be higher paying than a fast food job due to my skills and education. This explains why companies can't low-ball executives during the hiring process (no qualified candidate would accept such offers).

One commonly proposed way to limit executive pay would be through government-mandated income caps for executives. In response, most employees with executive skills will simply exercise their options: —some of them will retire (most CEOs are older), some will start their own companies to receive compensation as an owner and not an employee, but mostly, companies will begin to exploit creative accounting maneuvers to appropriately compensate high level executives (e.g.,. deferred stock compensation, gifting, and good old fashioned embezzling).

Do these people deserve their high pay? The question of who deserves what is philosophical, not scientific. Economics in most cases can only explain situations and the consequences or tradeoffs to society. Asking an economist the question "Is it fair for CEOs to earn so much money while employees at the same company earn so much less"? Is akin to asking a physician: "Is it fair that childhood cancers are more aggressive than adult cancers?" Economists and physicians can only offer awkward answers when faced with such philosophical questions.

Topic 10: In this economy where there are people with bachelor's and master's degrees taking minimum wage jobs, how can you argue that there is no need to raise the minimum wage?

I completely agree that there are too many people with advanced degrees working in minimum wage jobs. Is this a sign that an economy with a low minimum wage is only producing low paying jobs? Does this contradict my repeated statements that higher skills equal higher pay? NO.

Why are many well-educated people only able to find crappy low paying jobs? The answer is simple, look at their degree. Most are earning degrees in fields that their parents, friends, and even professors constantly joke, about how they will be jobless in the end. Fine Arts, English Literature, Music Therapy, Film, and Dance, among others. It's no mystery to any person who has a friend or family member earning low wages with an advanced degree about why that person is working a low paying job after college. They studied subjects that appealed to them without discovering and developing the skills employers actually demand and require. This is why a person with a graphic design degree is making around $15 an hour [11], while someone with a degree in computer engineering earns about double that [12]. This doesn't even account for what I'm sure is a vastly different employment rate between the two professions.

We should really only start to panic about the highly-educated being employed in large numbers at our burger joints when those people have degrees in subjects that are perpetually in demand – those in science, technology, engineering, or math (STEM careers). If our statement read "graduates with their bachelor's in engineering and computer programming are working at the local coffee shop then it's time to panic. It should come as no surprise that the only thing graphic designers are designing is a cappuccino.

Let's rephrase the concept about *skills* leading to high paying jobs. It's not about just having any old skill, it's about possessing and expertly wielding those skills that employers want. It is difficult to sell what people don't want to buy. Employers just aren't interested in purchasing labor from college graduates with unwanted and obsolete skill sets. This is fairly evident from the difficulty graduates in these worthless majors face when applying for jobs.

Topic 11: Most people making the minimum wage are adults and not teenagers starting out.

According to the U.S. Bureau of Labor Statistics, approximately half of the workers earning minimum wage are 24 or under; meaning the other half are older than 24 [1]! If that fact was all you absolutely knew about the demographics of minimum wage workers in the U.S., it would sound like most American adults are trapped in minimum wage jobs. Let's deconstruct this new knowledge with statistics that we have already established:

1. The minimum wage only affects about 4% of all American workers (~3.9%, refer to the section *"**Wouldn't employers just pay employees pennies for their labor, if there were no minimum wage enforced by the government**.*"

2. Approximately 50% of minimum wage earners are adults.

This means that only 2% of American adults earn minimum wage (4% x 50% = 2%). Not exactly what I would consider a cruel system that traps adults into minimum wage jobs. Moreover, a reasonable person would realize that there are significantly more people that can be categorized as adults than teenagers' and students'. Strictly speaking the group of younger workers only encompasses an 8 year period of life (24–16 = 8), whereas the adult worker group spans 53 years of life (78–25 = 53). Again then, why are half of minimum wage workers adults? There are a lot more adults than teenagers in this society. So even if the average adult worker is five times less likely to be working a minimum wage job, the fact that there are more than 5x the number of adults than teenagers would mean this is not an apples to apples comparison.

From a nerdy perspective I've heard from friends that White

people in the United States spend more money than Asian people on Japanese Cartoon DVDs in America. I haven't verified this to be true, but it wouldn't surprise me if this was the case. There are more people who fall into the category of White than Asian [4]. The average White person only has to be a fraction as likely to buy a particular item as an Asian person in the United States, to be the majority purchaser of that item. The point is if you want to compare statistics between groups, you need to account for the different group sizes to have any real-world implications.

Many try unsuccessfully to refute the fact that most minimum wage workers are teenagers by arguing that the "average age of those earning minimum wage is 35." This may be true, but only for those that can't comprehend basic math beyond the third grade. What do we learn in the fourth grade? There are three ways to determine central tendencies of data, namely mean, median, and mode. Some try to confuse and mislead the uninformed or uneducated by purposefully reporting one of these calculations to suit an agenda. Which calculated number is most likely to be the highest? Probably, the mean. Why? The range of ages is entirely too high for the center to be determined by mean to be accurate. Let's demonstrate why the calculations (and their subsequent reporting use) are so misleading:

Here are ten random numbers—16, 16, 17, 18, 19, 22, 35, 41, 56, 70.

Mean: To find the mean, add all of these numbers and divide them by the total amount of numbers. Adding all ten numbers equals 310. Now, divide 310 (sum) by 10 (total amount of numbers); the answer is **31** as our mean. Despite six of the numbers being at least 9 less than 31. This is obviously not a very accurate center point.

Mode: This is the easiest to calculate. The mode is the number that occurs most often. The mode in our number set is **16**.

Median: This is also easy to calculate. Order the number set from largest to smallest, then locate the number in the middle. The median in this case would actually be the mean of 19 and 22, since there are even amounts of numbers in our data set. The median in our example equals **20.5**.

As you can see, talking about "average" ages can be very misleading when discussing the minimum wage. *Common sense and basic observation make it obvious that a person is much more likely to be earning minimum wage as a young and inexperienced worker than they are as an older worker with experience.*

Topic 12: Why do you have such strong feelings against the minimum wage?

The minimum wage hurts the poor. This is easy to comprehend when we carefully examine the effects caused by minimum wage in America. In the working world, *skills* determine the wages people earn in the workplace. Skills that workers possess have influence on an employer's demand for their labor. The absolute reason minimum wage workers earn minimum wage is because they have little or no skills.

Where are poor people with low/no skills most likely to acquire skills that will lead to higher incomes? Are poorer workers going to obtain those skills at an expensive technical school or college? Or, will they acquire higher skills working for an employer where they will receive on-the-job training; thereby, build real-world experience? In reality, they will procure necessary and in-demand skills while on the job.

The minimum wage ensures difficulty when low-skilled people join the workforce. Employers place very little value on unskilled labor. If they value it below the present government-decreed minimum wage then most low/no-skilled jobs will be destroyed or simply, never created. Employers will NOT pay more than they know certain labor is worth. My point is clear - under a minimum wage law, it takes more time for those entering the workforce to gain skills on-the-job that will allow them to become skilled workers. Let me explain this argument with my own work history.

I began earning minimum wage when I was 17 working at a grocery store. The minimum wage then was $5.15 an hour. Following three months at that store and only receiving a $0.25 an hour raise, I began hunting for a better paying job so I could have more money to take the non-existent ladies in my life out for nice dates. I used the skills I gathered at the grocery store—using a

Point-of-Service gun for registering inventory, unloading delivery trucks, and using a pallet jack to move pallets around. These skills lead me to a warehouse job where I earned $9.50 an hour. There wasn't a chance in hell that the warehouse would have hired me without the experience and skills I brought from my short time at the grocery store.

Six months passed at the warehouse and there were no signs of any raise coming my way. Again, I searched for different opportunities. I was able to land a factory job making $15 an hour due to my experience with an electric fork lift, assembly line picking and materials handling experience I gained from the warehouse. After graduating from a university with a bachelor's in Economics, I was offered an entry-level supervisor position making $20 an hour. At the tender age of 23, I had accumulated a variety of marketable skills if I had wanted to stay in blue-collar jobs. You can see that through this process how I evolved from a worker with no skills, to become a skilled blue-collar worker in just a few short years - all while attending college full-time. My story isn't unique, most working American have similar stories about how they acquired skills to earn better pay.

My hardest job to land was the minimum wage job. It took 3 years to find an employer gave me my first job. Which employer was going to take the risk of losing money training a kid with zero work history? Especially if they had to pay the kid more than the labor is worth.

In my teen years, my friends and I would spend two weeks each year submitting job applications. Without a single job offer, we would be easily discouraged. If the minimum wage law wasn't in place, it would have been possible to negotiate with a business to make it easier to land a job. I'd plead with them, "Hey I'll work free for a week so you can test me out and see if I'm the kind of employee you want." Not many employers would turn down an offer like that. Once they saw that I was eager to learn and would show up on time every day, I have absolutely no doubt that they would have hired me with a paid job. For the employers that didn't hire me, at least I could talk about the short amount of work experience I got at my next job interview.

Instead, I was a kid with a lot of free time on my hands. What did I do with that free time? I'd drink cheap beer with my friends, loiter at businesses, and engage in dangerous drag races with my parent's car. What's that saying about idle hands?

I've got to ask the minimum wage supporters this question. Which scenario is more preferable?

1. A world with an *enforced* minimum wage? Wherein I was unable to find a job because employers thought, "This pimply kid with zero experience is simply not worth $5.15 an hour." This delayed my entry into the workforce until I was 17 - and I only landed the job after completing over a hundred job applications. This also encouraged a dangerous teenage drinking habit throughout the week since I had nothing productive to do.

2. A world *without* minimum wage - Wherein I could negotiate my own pay with employers and accept income below the minimum wage. I would have been able to land a job within my first few attempts because I would have negotiated for far less money. In that scenario I would have begun acquiring skills at the age of 14. I would have more opportunities to explore various jobs and industries while I was still young with limited responsibilities. And I probably wouldn't have been so reckless with alcohol, since the job would have occupied my free time.

Examining those two scenarios, it's no contest what would have been better. I feel robbed of so many different opportunities had I been able to negotiate for work at an earlier age. Advocates for the minimum wage are so vehemently focused on the specific hourly pay rate that they wholly ignore other benefits associated with employment – chiefly, the accumulation of valuable skills. Developing in-demand skills earlier will always position workers to achieve higher paying jobs in the future.

Chapter 2—Welfare

Topic 13: Good God, you seriously can't be against welfare programs, can you?

Welfare is the support offered by the government to poor and/or elderly people in a society. This usually comes in the form of direct monetary payments to the poor (welfare payments), credit for food (food stamps), retirement income guarantees (social security), and healthcare subsidies (Medicare, Medicaid, CHIP, health insurance exchanges, among others). With the exception of social security and Medicare, a person is only allowed to receive the aid after being "means tested"—which means when people apply for them, the administrators of the programs check the income of the applicant to make sure they are actually poor.

For countless generations, people have asked politicians from around the world to create programs that act like welfare to aid the poor. As a result, the politicians have set up policies of taxation to raise the money necessary to fund these programs. The objection most often raised with respect to welfare programs is that these programs cost the taxpayer too much money. I personally couldn't care less about the taxes. Instead, what I hate about welfare is what it does to the poor.

The stated intention of welfare is great—"Help those in dire financial situations lift themselves up out of poverty." I'm completely in support of that, and I volunteer at charities that aid the poor when I have the time. I honestly couldn't imagine a person who would be against the noble goal of helping the poor get on their feet.

However, when we actually take a good hard look at the effects of welfare, we can see that they keep the less fortunate in poverty and make the society as a whole poorer. This is the primary reason for my hatred of welfare. These claims get people up in arms anytime somebody brings it up. Unfortunately, economists have been very bad at communicating how and why bad things happen when we try to have government help out the little guy through welfare. My explanation in the following chapters will probably sound equally bad.

A secondary reason for why I personally despise welfare programs is the social strife these programs cause. Taxpayers are outraged that they have to work hard day in and day out only to have a portion of their income redirected to people who are not employed. Meanwhile, the poor and advocacy groups for the poor are disgusted with the fact that taxpayers are unsympathetic about the tragic plight experienced by the poor. These arguments usually crowd out the question I think is most important to address—does welfare actually help or hurt the poor?

Topic 14: How does welfare hurt the poor?

Welfare discourages people from taking the next step up the career/economic ladder and also discourages people from acquiring capital to invest in themselves. To explain my point that welfare prevents people from taking the next step up the career/economic ladder, I will use the following examples from my own personal life:

I have a friend named John Doe living on welfare, and he's been very candid with me about the benefits he receives from the government. Just to give you a little bit of background information on John, he is in his late twenties with a live-in girlfriend and a 3-year-old child. Let's do a rundown of the aid he and his family receive from the government, and it is as follows:

1. Section 8 Housing—John and his family live in an

apartment for which they pay $200 monthly in rent. These apartments normally go for a rent of $850 a month. When you do the math, $650 comes from his Section 8 voucher.

2. Food stamps—He and his family receive food stamps totaling around $320 monthly.

3. Welfare payments—it used to be $840 a month. I'm not sure if it's more now.

If we total it up, John is pulling in around $1,810 in benefits from various welfare programs (There are programs I'm probably missing in there). Let's say John was offered a full-time job that pays $10.10 an hour (the supposed living wage). Would he be better off in the short-term taking that job? No. In fact most people would advise John not to. If he were to take the job, he would run the risk of losing some or all the benefits he's receiving from the government, which at present is worth more than the living wage he would be offered to take the job. Most of John's friends and family couldn't bear to watch their loved one suffer in the labor market when he could earn more by being unemployed. Their misplaced compassion for John, coupled with the fact that the welfare option is available will probably result in them telling John to forego the job to keep the welfare.

You can do the math for yourself, and you'll see that the welfare package he and his family are receiving is going to be worth a bit more than the monthly wage of around $1,616 pre-tax that he would be earning from a job which pays $10.10 an hour (10.10 * 40 * 4 = 1,616). John is going to make the rational economic decision and delay taking up a job because of that. I don't judge his character at all. He's an excellent father to his kid. To tell you the truth, if I was in his exact same situation I would without a doubt stay on welfare too. It would be ridiculously stupid in the short-term to walk away from the guaranteed sources of government income, especially when the alternative is to take on the risk of getting a job at a lower benefit that may or may not pan out.

If John stays on welfare, his income is always going to be capped to what he can receive in government benefits. Meanwhile, John's friends (including me) who are still in the workforce are constantly gaining more and more skills in the workplace. As a result, the incomes of his friends continue to increase, given that these gains in skills continue as long as they're employed. John is always going to be left in the same situation as he was in when he started receiving welfare, while John's friends who've remained in the workforce have all accumulated considerable job skills and pay raises. As long as John qualifies for such a generous welfare package, he is going to continue being unemployed. In the long run, this scenario will keep John from finding high-paying work in the future, as his skills are not being developed at a job like his friends' skills are. Even if John wants to work it will be difficult to find a job that offers him a higher benefit than his welfare package, as he is not developing any skills while on welfare.

It's not just the poor who fall into this trap of having their ability to work and acquire skills capped. This happens to rich women who get married at a very young age and are forced out of the labor force. They and their partners make the decision that the women would stay at home with the kids and tend to the affairs of the house. If these women were ever to divorce their husbands, they will find themselves at risk for a financial catastrophe. The years they spent trapped at home guarantees that they will not have the skills to find a high-paying job after the divorce.

Let's move onto my second point on how welfare keeps the poor in a constant state of poverty. It discourages people from saving money to better themselves. Since the government doesn't want the wealthy or middle class receiving welfare or government assistance, a welfare applicant has to report not only their income to the government, but also their assets. The result is that most poor people will spend their money as quickly as they receive it, given that any savings they hold will count against them at the welfare office. Under this means tested system—How is a person supposed to save any money to go to school to get a better job? How are they supposed to save any money to cover the costs of moving to areas with a larger number of better-paying jobs? How are they supposed to save any money to buy a car to drive to job interviews?

Another problem with means-testing is that as welfare recipients have to send their bank statements in with their application for government assistance if they have bank accounts, they hide their assets in untraceable cash. The disadvantages of cash are that it diminishes in value, owing to inflation, and, more importantly, it leaves the people holding it very vulnerable to getting robbed in their homes or on the streets. In the past, I became aware that many people at the food pantry I used to volunteer at hoarded cash. They would come up to me to and ask if they could give me cash so that I could make an online purchase for them with my credit card. The reason why they do this is simple—they can't put their money in the bank where the government can see it while they are receiving benefits, and you need a debit or credit card to make online purchases.

Topic 15: What do economists mean when they say welfare keeps the poor dependent?

Welfare keeps the poor dependent for the exact reasons I laid out in my previous explanation. They are as follows:

1. Welfare incentivizes failure and punishes success—This is pretty self-explanatory. The less money you earn from working, the more benefits you get out of welfare. The reverse of that is the more money you earn working, the less benefits you receive from welfare programs. Therefore, people with no/low skills will act rationally in the short-term by maximizing their welfare benefits at the expense of acquiring skills that in the present have no immediate benefit to them.

2. <u>Means-tested programs prevents capital accumulation</u>—
Means-tested programs require you to meet specific income or lack of income requirements to qualify for them. We don't want rich people to receive food stamps or section 8 housing. Means-testing requires the poor to stay poor to receive government benefits. If you have savings in the bank for education or transportation that can improve your skills and lead to better-paying jobs in the future, it will reduce the benefits you receive from welfare. Welfare proponents may seek to counter this effect by asking the government to remove means-testing. However, you then run into a fiscal stability issue when the entire country goes to apply for government benefits.

This government assistance considered to do good has the effect of making sure that poor people don't acquire any skills on the job and that they don't save enough money to help them acquire qualifications that will help them find jobs. That's why a lot of economists say that these programs keep people poor and subsidizes failure. A person receiving welfare is pushed into trading the profitable long-term skills that could be gained on the job for meager short-term payments that keeps them poor forever. It would be irrational for them to work so long as the welfare benefits offered are more generous than the pay they can receive with their level of skill.

Topic 16: Foreign aid (welfare) helps starving kids around the world eat. Are you against giving aid to the poor?

We've explored how domestic welfare fails the people it intends to help. So it's no surprise that international welfare fails the less fortunate people in foreign countries as well. It's tragic because the reason international aid keeps people poor is the same reason domestic welfare keeps citizens poor. It prevents the citizens from acquiring skills on the job, and it prevents people from pooling capital to be more productive.

The American government and charity organizations spend tens of billions of dollars every year sending aid to help alleviate poverty in countries abroad. This aid usually comes in the form of money, food, supplies, among others. As we've seen time and time again, the bulk of this aid is usually stolen by the ruling elites or local warlords to both finance and supply their lavish lifestyles and current military campaigns. For the sake of simplicity though, we are going to focus on the effects of the aid that actually goes to the poor and starving in those developing countries. Let's explore this by envisioning a scenario where a fictional village receives welfare from generous foreigners.

In our fictional village, the local economy is made up of fisherman, farmers, and carpenters. A package each of grain and corn arrive one day that can supply the whole village for 3 months. The locals rejoice, and a fantastic party is thrown to celebrate this occasion.

The next morning the farmers go out to tend their fields. After a hard day of breaking their backs on the fields, they take the crops they've picked for sale outside their houses. This day is different though, as nobody stops by to purchase any of the crops they've picked. A couple of days pass, and one of the corn farmers decides to go out and find his usual customers and inquire why they're not coming around anymore to purchase his corn. He finds the wife of a local fisherman and asks why she hasn't stopped by for her usual bushel of corn. She gives him a stare and says, "Haven't you heard the good news? The foreigners have sent us enough free corn and grain to last for 3 months, why would I buy any food from you farmers then?" The farmer replies back "That's awesome for the village, but what about my farm?" The woman responds with an apathetic shrug. A couple of weeks later, all the farmers are out of business. How can they sell their corn if somebody is giving away the same food for free all day, every day? Now in the village there are no longer any farmers. The fact is that they are not going to break their backs in the field, growing crops no one will buy.

Three months pass, and the same village receives another provision of corn and grain. It is accompanied by a 3-month supply of preserved fish this time. The local people rejoice, and another killer party is thrown to celebrate this occasion. The next morning, the fishermen go out to catch fish. As usual, after a hard day of fishing and getting sunburned, they take the fish they've picked for the day and place them for sale outside their houses. This day is different though, as nobody stops by to purchase any of the fish they've caught. A couple of days pass, and one of the fishermen asks his wife to go out and find one of his usual customers and inquire why they're not coming around anymore to purchase his fish. She finds one of the men who used to farm for corn, and asks why he hasn't been around to buy any of her husband's fish. He gives her a stare and says, "Haven't you heard the good news? The foreigners have sent us enough preserved fish to last for 3 months; why would I buy any food from you fishermen then?" The wife of the fisherman replies back, "That's awesome for the village, but what about my husband's fishing business?" And to that she receives no reply from the man she had turned her back on the previous month. A couple of weeks later, all the fishermen are out of business, as they can't sell their fish because somebody is giving away fish for free all day, every day. Now along with not having farmers in the village anymore, you also no longer have any fishermen in the village. Why would the fishermen go out and get sunburned all day to catch fish that nobody's going to pay them for?

As demonstrated above, when you give people free stuff all day, every day, you crush the local industry that is currently providing the free goods or services you're handing out in exchange for nothing. Industries will no longer continue to manufacture products, unless they have paying customers. If they do decide to just give out their merchandise for free, how are they going to purchase any of the materials they need to produce their finished product (in the above example, they would be farm tools and fishing rods)? What would their motivation be for getting their bodies beat up from farm work or sunburned from fishing? If I were in their situation, I would just laze around and hang out with family and friends all day, living off the free stuff the foreigners were sending to the village.

Let's go back and check on our fictional village and see what else is happening. A few more days pass after the second package of aid is delivered, and one of the local villager's roofs collapses completely and is in need of repair. They call the town carpenter to fix the roof. Unfortunately for them, she's out of business too. Why? What's her motivation for gathering supplies and climb onto a ladder? She doesn't care if they give her fish or grains, as she can get them for free. Why should she gather wood in the forest, climb onto a ladder, and sweat it out, constructing somebody's roof if all they have to give her is something that she can already get for free?

In the village, even an industry that isn't forced into direct competition with free aid supplies usually either stops production or drastically decreases in production. Why would they produce goods or offer services, if there's nothing anybody can offer them that they can't already get for free? That's why it's not likely that the people in our fictional village are ever going to progress past the point of poverty in that system. Basically, all that will be consumed will be the aid provided by foreigners.

In the end, the foreign aid stops the local people from acquiring any skills. They're discouraged from working as there's no incentive for them to work. It stops businesses from accumulating capital. Why would you buy farm tools, fishing rods, fishing boats, among others, to produce products that you literally have to give away for free to get rid of? In the end, their economy will never have the chance to grow and branch out into different industries.

As a side note, this wouldn't work in a country as developed as the United States. If you offered grain and fish for free, while being able to distribute that out for free as well, you would bankrupt the fish and grain industry. But it wouldn't cripple our country as a whole because we have a very large and diverse economy due to our accumulated capital. The people from the bankrupt industries would just go to an area where we sorely need workers, such as the petroleum industry. The reason why free stuff affects poor countries so much more than the rich ones is because they don't have the capital to produce or distribute other goods or services yet. Very poor countries usually only have a few industries to begin with. They are usually industries that don't require a lot of capital to produce things. That's why those countries have industries that are usually based on agriculture, hunting, and fishing. They just don't have the accumulated resources to do anything else at that stage of development.

Topic 17: Don't corporations receive more welfare from the government than poor people?

That depends entirely on how you ask the question. If you're asking, "Do American corporations as a whole receive more welfare from the American government than private citizens?" Then the answer is no. If you're asking, "Do American corporations individually receive more money than individual welfare recipients?" Then the answer is yes. Corporations as a whole received about $100 billion in 2014 from the federal government [5], while Medicaid alone cost around $476 billion in 2014 [6]. Why do corporations individually receive more money than individual Americans? It's just because corporations are comprised of a lot of people.

In any case, I see a lot of angry people who bring up the fact that corporations receive welfare too. I'm with them in the need for us to get rid of those subsidies. Those subsidies cause a lot of manipulation in the market (i.e. the business that gets the subsidies will be able to have an unfair competitive advantage over those that don't). What I don't like is that people who are against corporate subsidies turn around and use this to try to justify the welfare for needy people—two wrongs don't make a right. Corporate subsidies create moral hazards that reduce overall production, and welfare does not help alleviate people out of poverty.

Topic 18: Is there any form of aid that actually works?

Private charity tends to be the best option to combat poverty. Charity isn't really means-tested, as they don't really require proof that you're poor to give you free food, shelter for the night, free healthcare (via free clinics), among others. This means that people are able to acquire capital and job skills, while still receiving aid from these private organizations. It doesn't really discourage work because the bulk of the services provided will only provide you sustenance and nothing more.

People are completely outraged that I would recommend private charity over government assistance. "How is a person who gets food from a soup kitchen better off in the long run than a person who collects food stamps?" is the common response I hear. The difference between the two is the food stamps coupled with other government welfare programs can serve as an easy substitute for working. Whereas subsisting off charity is a horrible experience that will keep you alive, but it'll never discourage work. Most people on charity would want to get out of that situation as quickly as possible. You can live off the charitable organization, but given the unpleasant nature of the facilities, it really is a last resort. To understand the difference, you have to take a look at how you receive the actual aid from the government in comparison to private charity.

Food—To get food from the government, you can apply for food stamps with an application that you can submit online. If you meet all the qualifications, you'll receive a monthly stipend for food on a plastic card, which will be accepted at most local grocery stores and some convenience stores. To get food from a private charity, you have to show up every day at certain time frames to get a hot meal at a facility which is not pleasant to be at. The stench in the air at these places can be overwhelming, and the people a bit off-putting. You can also go to a local food bank at certain times of the week to pick out food from a general pantry, which has very limited food choices.

Shelter—To get shelter from the government, you can apply for a Section 8 housing voucher at a U.S. Department of Housing and Urban Development Office (HUD). If you qualify for this program, the government will pay your landlord a fixed amount monthly, with you covering the difference if there is any. To get shelter from charity, there's no checking of income. You just have to show up between certain times at a facility that houses the homeless. You'll most likely be sharing the room you sleep in with a large number of very shady strangers. In the morning, the shelter usually forces you out, so you can engage with society (also they need the space for other public services). There are more long-term housing solutions as well. One alternative would be to live in a halfway house with some very unsavory characters.

Cash—You can apply for either unemployment or the Temporary Assistance for Needy Families Program (TANF). If you qualify, you will receive a check or direct deposit from the government. To receive cash from a charity is very rare, and I'm unaware of any ways to receive a steady cash flow from a charity, except when one is a disabled veteran.

Healthcare—You can get Medicaid by applying online via the Healthcare.Gov website or by visiting their local office. Once you are approved, you will receive an insurance card that works the same way as a private insurance (i.e. they'll have a list of private doctors to choose from, and some cost sharing may be applicable). To obtain healthcare from private charities, you usually have to apply at the clinic through an application that's somewhat similar to the Medicaid application. They will then allow you to schedule appointments or walk-in for both preventative and urgent care. The downside of private charity is the waiting time is often very long, and the face-to-face time one receives with a physician is usually very short.

Assuming you are poor enough to be receiving aid from a

private charity, you probably will qualify for all the government aid mentioned above. Do you see the difference between receiving aid from the government and receiving aid from private charities? Getting aid from a charity is less desirable in comparison to the government option. A person has to go daily to the area where the aid is being dispensed to get food and shelter and have to be around people they wouldn't want to normally be around. The person receiving government aid basically gets funds from the government to use at their own discretion. They are allowed to choose where they want to live and which grocery store they want to shop at.

Most people would say that the government option is the best, as it makes life easier for the recipients. Government aid is always easier to obtain and much more generous than private charity. Unfortunately, the government welfare makes life so easy for the poor in comparison to their alternative options that it disincentives people from working. What is their motivation for working if they have material security while not having to do anything to obtain it? It's like God hitting up each and every gym in the world and saying, "Hey bros, I'm going to change how your biology works. I'm going to grant everyone on the planet with a decent beach body." How many people would you expect to see working hard and sweating it out at any gym a year later?

Let's be honest here, for the most part, work is awful. It is hard to wake up early and leave your family to go to a place where you'll be told to do stuff all day, by a boss who you might think is an asshole. That's why I don't trust a person who says they would do their job for free. While work has its downsides, the benefits from work far outweigh the negative aspects associated with it. You gain skills on the job, forge lifelong connections, and receive money at the end of your pay period. The problem with welfare is that it provides one of the benefits of working (getting paid), without a person ever having to go to a job, and therefore they miss out on gaining skills. This results in a standard of living that will always be capped at what you can receive in government benefits, which isn't a lot.

A doctor doesn't want their patients to live entirely sedentary lifestyles because it's comfortable, and an economist doesn't want people to be away from work for too long because welfare makes it comfortable to live without a job. Both scenarios lead to decay in the long-term. The sedentary lifestyle rots your body, and welfare rots your job skills. I want the first option for a down and out person to be seeking employment. The last option should be turning to a third party for aid. Charity accomplishes this, and even though you can survive off it, it's awful to do so. On the flip side, welfare makes it much easier to be poor.

Topic 19: Without minimum wage, welfare, and all the other protections provided by the government, Americans would be as poor as people in developing countries.

This is an example of reverse thinking. Americans aren't rich because of the laws that enable minimum wages and welfare. Those laws were put into place after we established ourselves as one of the richest countries in the world. If making a country rich just required lawmakers in those countries to make rules controlling the wages employers had to pay to employees and that wealth would be redistributed to the poor to allow them to succeed, every country in the world would be as wealthy as the United States. In fact, almost all countries have tried both the strategies at one point or another. As a result, they ended up with the same situation we see in the United States—the systemic long-term poverty among their low-skilled workers. Unfortunately for developing countries, they have a much higher population of unskilled workers than the developed countries. Which means most of their population is poor.

The quick and easy answer to why we see the wealth disparity between the United States and a country such as Vietnam is that there is a huge productivity gap between the workers in both countries. Americans are a lot wealthier than the Vietnamese because American workers are a lot more productive than Vietnamese workers. An average American worker produces about 8 times more goods and services as measured by value, than the average Vietnamese worker [7].

Before you get the wrong idea, American workers aren't 8 times more productive than the Vietnamese workers because we're 8 times stronger, faster, or 8 times more intelligent than the workers in Vietnam. An American worker might be a better performer all else equal, but it's not nearly enough to account for the income difference when compared to their Vietnamese counterpart.

Why is the productivity of these two groups of workers so different if the physical and mental capacities of both the groups are pretty similar? It's because the Americans have access to a lot more capital than the Vietnamese. In other words, the Vietnamese workers don't have the equipment and machinery that make American workers so unbelievably productive. Instead of producing a few pair of jeans per hour with sewing machines like they do in Vietnam, the American factory workers use industrial garment presses to turn out hundreds of pairs of jeans per hour. Instead of using farm animals to plow a few acres of land a week, the American farmers use tractors that can do the same in an hour. Instead of using bikes and small trucks to deliver packages, the American delivery services use planes, trains, and trucks the size of houses to move billions of packages every year.

The solution for how to end Vietnamese poverty is simple.

They need to increase the amount of capital in their country so that they can use machines instead of just raw labor to be more productive. There are two ways for them to do that, and they are as follows:

1. The first way is for them to divert some of their resources away from consumer goods (food, clothing, shelter, among others) to purchase capital goods (factory machines, tractors, trucks, among others). That's not a very popular move in a country where people are literally living in constant hunger.

2. The second way is for them to have foreigners invest in their economy by building factories, which increasingly become more advanced as the economy grows and matures. This move is also not very popular as the wages the factory workers earn are often called slave wages by the citizens in the country that sends over the equipment. Even though the wages the Vietnamese earn at these factories are often

higher than anything they can earn anywhere else in their country.

The only way for a country to develop is by making themselves more productive through the use of machinery and equipment. That's why I stated before that I hate aid for poor countries. As well intentioned as it is, the aid prevents countries from accumulating capital, just like how welfare prevents people from accumulating capital. Fortunately, despite the unpopularity of the two capital accumulation methods, Vietnam has finally started to embrace both of them. As a result, the average Vietnamese income has been growing year after year. Will their incomes catch up with that of the Americans in the near future? Probably not. Growing from a poor developing country to an industrial super power is not an overnight process.

Chapter 3—Corporate Profit

Topic 20: The high profit of corporations is definitive proof that Americans are being robbed blind!

I have never understood the reasoning behind this popular line of thinking touted by politicians. Are they saying that if some businesses or persons earns a lot of money, then they're automatically doing something wrong and illegal? It seems to me that this is just blind outrage without any rhyme or reason behind it. If these corporations are making insane profits by engaging in illicit and illegal activity, please bring some evidence of that so we can get the authorities involved. I am sure there are a few corporations that engage in some illegal activities to spike their balance sheets, and they should be dealt with under the law. However, the vast majority of companies have to earn their money legitimately by offering some goods or services to the buyers. These buyers are perfectly willing to pay for something that makes their lives that much better. The reason why a small number of companies earn an obscene amount of money is a testament to the huge demand they encounter for their products coupled with their continued ability to supply those products to the people.

ExxonMobil is a company that has consistently been featured among the top most profitable companies in America [8]. Exxon earns most of their money by extracting oil from the ground and refining that oil into gasoline, petrochemicals, and other miscellaneous petroleum products. It should be pretty clear why Exxon earns a ton of money. They operate in the oil markets, and people all around the world are dependent on oil consumption for their day-to-day activities (I'm not about to get into a debate on global warming here), so the demand is there. Oil is very difficult and costly to extract from the ground and refine, so there is less competition from other suppliers. If you look at how Exxon actually operates, you'll realize pretty quickly that this corporation earns their money the hard way.

1. To produce any of their refined oil products, Exxon has to
   hire huge teams of geologists to hunt for areas that have oil
   resources.

2. Once an oil field is located, they have to pay a team of
   lawyers and additional scientists to study the environmental
   impact, assess risk, and compile safety proposals.

3. Once all that is done, they have to set up a local
   infrastructure around the field for the operations. This
   might include roads to help transport supplies and
   electricity generating stations to power all the heavy
   equipment they'll be using.

4. Then they finally bring in the rigs to drill their first holes.
   These rigs cost millions of dollars, with an additional cost
   of tens of thousands for transport to their respective fields.
   From there a crew of drillers drill test holes to see if there is

actually any oil there. Some of these areas will turn out to have little or no oil at all. If this is the case, the oil company loses millions of dollars (all in the cost of doing business).

5. If the field in fact possesses a large amount of recoverable oil, then the oil company builds more permanent infrastructure. This infrastructure will be used to supply the operation with the equipment necessary to extract the oil from the ground. Pipelines and additional roads are then created to carry the oil out of the field.

6. The extracted oil is then transported out in huge tankers, pipelines, or trains to an oil refinery that is hundreds if not thousands of miles away.

7. Once the oil arrives at the distillery (facilities the size of small towns), it is placed in large machines that heat it up to vaporize and separate the oil into many different petroleum products. This process is called fractional

distillation.

8. Once this is done, the finished products are transported to processing plants to get them ready to be turned into final products such as gasoline, cooking fuels, waxes, among others.

9. Then the finished goods are transported out to be sold at wholesale and retail locations around the world.

All the work Exxon puts into making sure there is gas for you to drive your car, gas to heat your home, and gas to cook your food, etc. is why they earn a ton of money. There is a high demand for their products, and they go to great extents to make sure they're able to supply it to their consumers. If people understood the steps it takes for businesses to produce the goods and services that they consume on a daily basis, they would be more understanding of why there is nothing wrong with a business earning considerable profits at the end of the day. If corporations weren't earning profit for all the hard work they put into their operations, they simply wouldn't operate, and everyone would be much poorer because of it. When you look at how much total product Exxon sells, you can see pretty clearly that Exxon doesn't really keep that much money at the end of the day. They keep less than ten cents of every dollar they earn as profit [8]. Why do their profits run to tens of billions then? Because the amount of goods they produce is astronomical.

Topic 21: Well isn't it still wrong for the wealthy to keep any
money at all from the profits they earn?

Billionaires live "billionaire lifestyles", not "billion-dollar lifestyles." When you actually look at their expenses and what they're spending their money on, it's rare to see them have non-financial assets that equal up to a sizeable percentage of their wealth. Their money is mostly used to help advance the plight of the lower/middle class via investment. Do they care about the little guys? Probably not any more or less than any of us care about other strangers. What they care about is making money and the only way for them to do that is to engage in or associate themselves in places that create value (the production of goods and services).

The pursuit of profit is not a bad thing. It drives people to produce the goods and services that others want to consume. It's basically a reward for giving people what they want, and you don't have to care about any one of the people you're serving. You just have to care about making money. The pursuit of profit leads to goods and services being produced and creates jobs for producing these goods and services. The most important thing that profit allows a society to do is permit individuals to pursue their own interests within the confines of economic realities, as opposed to being forced into a collective to serve the greater good as defined by the whims of whoever wields government power at the time.

Topic 22: Since the wealthy own the capital, isn't it impossible for ordinary citizens to gain wealth and get ahead?

Let's break down the premise of the argument that wealth is hoarded by the wealthy people, and that wealth is essentially passed down through the generations via inheritance alone. A world in which wealth is kept by only a few individuals would mean that people outside a select number of families would not be able to gain any wealth in their working lives. This would result in the poor and middle class being unable to pass on anything to their children for them to get ahead, thus repeating the entire cycle of money accumulating in the hands of a few.

This argument is predicated on the idea that wealth can actually be hoarded in a system of voluntary exchange (free markets). The problem is that the wealthy can't get away with that in such a scenario.

1. Are they not going to loan any of their money out via bank deposits or investments?

2. Are they not going to hire any workers to work in their factories?

3. Are they not going to purchase any goods in the market from poor or middle class citizens?

If they do any of the above-mentioned activities, their wealth cannot be hoarded. Let me explain the results of the three above-mentioned actions in the following sections:

1. They loan their money out via bank deposits or investments. When a wealthy person deposits their money in a bank or invests it directly into the financial market, the money gets funneled to somebody who has a need for it. Once the money is put in the bank, it immediately gets lent

out by the same bank to be put to work by people who take out a loan. Those borrowers can in turn use that money to build a new business or expand an existing one. Or they can use it to purchase consumer goods to increase the quality of their lives (via cars, houses, to name a few). If the money is invested in the market, it will be used by a business to start or expand their operations. In either case, the money is not left idle in some vault, if it was it would be eroded by inflation. The excess money of the wealthy is almost always lent out to better the lives of people who have ideas on how to use that money productively or need the money to finance a purchase to improve their standard of living.

2. Hiring workers to work in their factories—I don't care how low the starting wages are, within a few years and by amassing skills with each job, a person will eventually be able to demand a higher salary. Eventually, they will reach a point where they can acquire their own capital.

3. They purchase goods and services—Not every business is owned by heirs and heiresses. A lot of new businesses are actually started by people who after financing their new business barely have two nickels to rub together. If the wealthy spend any money in the economy, that money will eventually find itself in the register of the local shopkeeper, if he puts out a product that people would want at a price they find reasonable.

From my own personal life my family took advantage of the economic mobility this great country has to offer the poor. They came to the U.S. after leaving a country that went into the hands of the communists. They didn't speak English, had job skills that didn't transfer well to jobs in this country, and like in most cases were stigmatized as foreigners. They were about as poor as one could get. That's why the first jobs they took, like a lot of Asian immigrants in this country, was work that paid below the minimum wage (under the table). At those jobs, they learned English by interacting with customers, they learned how small businesses operated in this country, and were able to network with other people. They used the skills they gained to get better-paying jobs at factories until they were able to save enough money to open their own businesses. The whole transition from poor refugees to the middle class took very little time for them. My grandparents retired comfortably, and the majority of my family now earns very respectable incomes.

To recapitulate, they took advantage of the fact that wealthy people hire others, and that the wealthy purchase goods and services to build wealth for them and their families. How would that journey from dirt poor refugee to affluent first world citizens be possible if the wealthy hoarded their wealth?

You can counter this argument with the statement, "your family's example is the exception and not the rule". But then I would just respond by showing you that the majority of the Asian

Americans who come from third world countries, usually as poor refugees, out-earn a wide number of Americans born into the middle class and wealthy families of America. We see this actually being played out in a lot of immigrant groups from different nationalities. As long as hard work is embedded in their culture, they could come to this country with nothing and end up making a fantastic living for themselves and their families. That's why America has so many successful East Asian small business owners, Indian doctors, Nigerian businessmen, Middle Eastern computer programmers, all who've lived through poverty most people couldn't imagine, raking in six or seven figures when they come to our free country. When we look at the incomes of Americans from East Asian, Indian, or Nigerian descent, it is evident that they have higher incomes than average native born Americans who had more wealth available to them growing up[9].

On the macro level, the fact that wealth can't be hoarded is also the reason why very poor countries have been able to increase their national incomes in the recent years. If income was completely limited to past wealth accumulation, countries like China and India would not be posting such staggering yearly gains in income. The relatively recent change from command economies to more market oriented economies has led to a boom in production in these economies. One of the most important ways these poor countries has been able to gain wealth is by attracting international investments from developed countries like the United States (i.e. taking advantage of the investments from the rich that we talked about earlier). The wealth that is supposedly hoarded by the wealthy in developed countries has in fact been invested into factories and jobs in poor countries. The exposure to foreign capital during the production cycle in these once poor countries is increasing the quantity and quality of skills in these poor countries. The exposure to foreign capital has been so successful for them that they've been able to create their own businesses that produce goods and services to sell back to the citizens of the wealthy countries. This economic activity has led to unprecedented gains in the material standard of living for those living in developing countries.

The flaws of the view that wealth can be hoarded are as follows:

1. It discounts one of the most valuable sources of production—human capital.

2. It portrays wealth as static and not fluid.

3. It mistakes those who own the capital for those who use the capital to better their own lives. For example, the company owners own all the machinery in a factory. However, the workers use that machinery to gain skills on the job to increase their own productivity. This results in their ability to get better pay in the future and possibly eventually start a business of their own.

History has shown that if the wealthy people don't use their wealth to be productive, they'll join the ranks of the poor. If we track the money of people who have held wealth for a long period of time, we see the vast majority of them actively investing in their own or other businesses. On the opposite end of the spectrum, rich people who don't invest the bulk of their money in productive activities tend to find themselves bankrupt pretty quickly.

The best example I can think of for groups of people not investing their wealth in productive areas and losing it is lottery winners. Just about every day somebody wins a big lottery, transforming their lives from piss poor to unfathomably wealthy. A large proportion of these people end up broke because the money is spent on lavish lifestyles with nothing going into productive investments. No matter how much money you have, nobody is immune from going broke. These lotto winners go from riches to rags in a heartbeat, as they spend all their money on consumption, without diverting their wealth to others to do productive things with.

Topic 23: Doesn't profit take money out of the hands of consumers?

Money is taken out of the pockets of the consumers once they choose to purchase goods and services produced by a company. Of course, the money's no longer with the original consumer. The fact that businesses earn profit will make the consumers' lives much better in the long run. Profits that a business earn will get reinvested into the production process to make the operations more efficient and cheaper, which will lower the future prices that consumers pay for existing goods and services. Corporate profit will also be used to do research and development, allowing companies to bring new products to the market.

I think what most people mean when they pose the question—

"Doesn't profit take money out of the hands of consumers?"—is actually "Does profit limit the amount of goods and services available to the entire society for consumption?" The answer is yes, it does limit the amount of goods and services for consumption in the short term. But it expands the available amount of goods and services people can consume in the long run. This is because the lion's share of the profit is usually funneled away from consumer spending into spending on capital (machinery equipment, facility expansion, among others) after the owners of the capital take a small bit out to consume (to buy those yachts and mansions that people are outraged about).

The three options each individual corporation and capital owner have when profit is made is to consume the profit by buying stuff for their own personal consumption, use that profit to repair and maintain their existing capital, or use that profit to invest in new capital. If you want to take a look at what these corporations actually do with their profit, take a look at the financial statements of the individual firms or just look at the dynamic growth in the size of their operations. From that, you'll see that the vast majority of the companies re-invest heavily for maintaining existing capital and purchasing new capital. This re-investment in capital increases productivity, leading to more goods and services being produced in the future. More goods and services being produced lead to increased consumption.

If a company were to price their goods at the cost it takes to produce them, they would be out of business in a heartbeat (or rely on donations to keep afloat). The reason is there would be no excess capital to grow or even maintain their current operations. Without profit where would the money come from to purchase a second store, or buy a new truck, or purchase a new sign? The excess profit companies earn is the engine for which businesses expand their operations leading to efficiencies in production and expansion of the goods and services they offer.

Chapter 4: Personal Subsidies

Topic 24: What harm do you see in helping students pay for their college education?

The song remains the same for me on the issue of aid to college students, as it's not the cost imposed on the taxpayer that I'm upset with, it is the effects of these actions on those who it's intended to help. In this case, when we try to make college education more affordable for students, we create massive long-term consequences for poor students. What ends up happening is rapidly rising tuition fees, unbelievably high student loan balances, and more often than not 2 to 8 years of the valuable time of the students are wasted on worthless degrees.

The government subsidizes the cost of education by

providing direct federal loans and low interest subsidized loans to borrowers, giving out grants, and by creating legislation to increase the willingness of lenders to give private loans to students. All of these options except for the private loans are presented to the student as soon as they fill out a Free Application for Student Aid (FAFSA) form. There is not a single American who can say that the government is not doing a lot to make sure that students can pay for college. Unfortunately that help is leading to huge problems for those students. This help comes in the form of:

Direct loans to borrowers—The borrower borrows the money from the United States government instead of a bank.

Interest subsidized loans—The student borrows from a private lender, but the government pays the interest on the loan while the borrower is attending college.

Favorable legislation on private loans—The government makes it pretty hard to get out of your student loans (i.e. the loans follow you even after declaring bankruptcy) and will even result in wage garnishments to get the money back for the bank if you stop paying. How is this supposed to help the borrowers? It entices lenders to make a lot of loans and also to charge lower interest rates. Without this guarantee of repayment, the private student loan market would shrivel up like a raisin. Why? Because with the guarantee, lenders can't really lose money on student loans, as they use the U.S. government as their collection agency. This is the reason it's easier to get approved for 100K in student loans than to get approved for a 5K car loan. The banks can lose money on a car loan if you don't pay, but it's almost impossible for the bank to lose money on the student loan. With respect to the student loans, they can send the government after you to collect if you don't pay.

Grants—Gives free money to those who have financial need. This is not a loan, so it never has to be repaid.

The problem is that making it easier to get student loans makes people behave in ways they otherwise wouldn't or couldn't. Without all this government intervention in the market, no bank in their right mind would lend people tens if not hundreds of thousands of dollars to study social work, art, liberal arts (or even to attend college as an undeclared major). They would be thinking, "There's no way this borrower is ever going to be able to pay us back with the average salary in these fields. They'll probably declare bankruptcy to escape paying back these loans."

Since the government uses the taxpayer's money instead of their own, they could not care less who they make direct loans to. It's not their money, and they are not going to care if they lose it. The only factor that prevents the government from making more of these kinds of loans is the concern of national debt.

The private lenders, on the other hand, are given a government guarantee that they are going to get repaid no matter what happens. That's why the interest rate on a student loan is the same for a philosophy major and engineering major. Even though the risk of getting paid back (without the government legislation) is so obviously different. Why is the risk different? Because those pursuing engineering degrees are much more likely to land a better-paying job after school than the philosophy major. Banks price out interest rates depending on risk—the riskier a loan is, the higher the interest rate. In the case of student loans, the government equalizes the risk of every student loan to the banks because there is almost no chance of any student getting out of paying the bank back.

Jill or Joe American can now get approved for student loans to study anything at any university they get accepted to. This removes one of the most powerful market checks on long-term failure, which is a people's unwillingness to risk losing their money to finance another person's pipe dreams. You can't walk into a bank and ask for a loan to start a business when you have no clue what you'll be producing. The market places checks on you by the bank declining the loan application if you lack the credentials. The people in government are willing to lend to any student who meets their income standards, and they've removed the risks on the banks to do the same. This makes it possible for students to take out tens of thousands of dollars in student loans to start an undergraduate program even if one doesn't know what they'll be studying (undeclared majors).

This has created a tragic situation where people become burdened with debt to study something that is interesting to them, but has no chance of landing them a job after school. We have huge sections of the youth laden with debt heading straight to low paying jobs. The society told them to study the subjects that would make them happy, then the politicians made sure that borrowed cash would continually rain down from the heavens to allow them to do the same. In the free market, there is no bank in this country that would allow students to commit that kind of financial suicide. This is not because they care about the youngsters, but because it would affect their pocketbooks when these artists, philosophers, and sociologists end up as baristas who default on their loans. In a free market young people would be more willing to stop and think,

"Why are so many people refusing to lend me money to study art?

Perhaps, I should think about whether or not to go to college now?

What can I study that will actually pay my bills?"

Topic 25: What's wrong with student grants then? Even if the students don't get jobs, they'll at least get a good education.

Let's ignore the elephant in the room to make the argument easier for the opposition; *It would cost the taxpayer enormous sums of money to send every kid to college for free.* The problem with sending kids to school for free is that they will be in almost the same situation as those who took out student loans—a lot of them will study subjects that interests them, instead of subjects they need to study in order to get a job, which is basically anything related to Science, Technology, Engineering, and Math (STEM). The only difference is that they won't have tuition linked debt to worry about.

One of the positive aspects of current government intervention in the finance of higher education is that we now know what people study when you give them enough grants to cover their education or easy financing. A great many of them study what they love and those are the fun subjects that have a slim chance of paying off down the road. The only time in their lives that these students are most likely to use this education is in the classroom and in casual conversations trying to impress a group of people. Let's face it, companies aren't going to come banging on the doors of philosophy majors with job offers.

In a world where education is free, students would soon realize that four years of free education isn't quite free at all. Despite not paying any tuition, they would pay high **opportunity costs** to attend schools in order to study worthless majors.

Opportunity Costs

1. *Missed opportunities to acquire real world skills*—If a student is studying full-time, they're probably not working

a full-time job. They get loaded up with worthless education, and give up real world job skills they could be earning with the same amount of time. Students often graduate schools with resumes that have nothing of value for most employers.

2. *Debts for living expenses*—Even if your tuition is being paid for by somebody else, a student still has to eat and be sheltered during their time at school. A lot of the debt that students incur is associated not only with tuition, but also the cost of living.

3. *Wasting the buffer of time young adults have to experiment with options*—One of the best things about being in your late teens and early twenties is that you have a lot of time and space to experiment and screw up. You are more likely to have limited responsibilities (i.e. no kids or expensive financial obligations.). Couple that with the likelihood that

your parents are probably still able to provide you with some support when you fail financially. This is the best time to take risks to figure out what areas you can best earn a living in. Students wasting their time with a useless field of study will not have the time to try different jobs to develop skills.

If you're able to study something in a field with good job prospects (such as STEM), then the opportunity costs can be easily payed for. Unfortunately, the majors most people head to, in the unchecked environment of easily financed higher education, is closely linked to barista jobs and poverty. It is never worth the outrageous tuition prices and, more importantly, the high opportunity costs associated with such degrees. This signals the fact that more than four years is wasted exploring various useless majors in university. The reality of this situation leads me to believe that no matter what the politicians say and what people want to believe—FREE COLLEGE WOULD BE A DISASTER!

Topic 26: How will students be able to pay for college if politicians don't help them?

College is so expensive these days as a result of the ways in which we've tried to help students finance college through the government. If you compare the historical cost of higher education to most other industries, you'll see that the cost of college has climbed much faster than just about every other consumer good or service. I personally find it amusing that the media never gets it right when they ask the question, "Why does the cost keep going up?" Just look into the financial statements of any of these colleges, and you can see where all the money's going.

Walk into any college campus today, and you'll be astounded at how opulent the infrastructure is compared to other modern facilities. Million-dollar stadiums, swimming pools, and state of the art research labs that are only used by a fraction of the student population—this is what's driving up the costs of college education today. Most of these colleges' financial statements will show that a lot of colleges spend less than half of their revenue on the salaries paid to professors'. This is insane, considering that almost of the learning is directly facilitated by these people. The bulk of the growth in tuition fees is directed towards wasteful ventures if useful education is the goal. Why waste so much money on these seemingly frivolous expenses? It's a great marketing tool to have such great student facilities and services when prospective students tour the campuses. Considering the number of students interested in higher education owing to the easy government financing, it is in a school's best interest to attract as many students as possible. Every school in every state is booming with business. Schools will continue to waste money, as long as the money is coming from student financing subsidies. Without the guarantee of the money flooding universities from the government, they would have to be cost conscious so they will bring down their price tags for students shopping around. I think we'd all be amazed at how much the cost of college would plummet if we got the government out of financing education.

The way people are going to pay for higher education is the same way they do now. They're going to pay out of their own pockets for what they can afford. Then they're going to take out loans for the remaining they can't afford. The key difference is that the people who need to take out loans will be forced to major in subjects that have a high chance of paying off (such as STEM), or they'll be denied the loans that could possibly ruin their futures. The biggest change of all is that colleges will become much cheaper. Schools will have to cut prices and rein in the spending on non-essential items such as student living luxuries and events to attract cost sensitive students to "study" at their universities

Topic 27: Are you saying that only the children of rich parents should be able to study whatever subject they want to? While the children of poor parents will have to study only the subjects that banks will help finance? How is that in the least bit fair?

Yes, that is exactly what I'm saying. The children of the rich can afford to fail. They have their parent's money and influence to fall back on if their degrees don't help them find a decently paying job. We've already established that in a free market, banks will only finance college majors that have a high success rate of finding jobs, since the banks want to get paid back. For college majors that are notoriously bad at preparing students for decently paying jobs, the only way to pay for them should be to do it out of one's own pocket. For the people concerned with income inequality, the fastest way to even out the gap is to have rich kids go to school for worthless majors, while at the same time have poor kids only going to school to learn subjects they can earn a living out of.

I can't see anything fairer then having rich parents finance their own kids to fail in subjects like art and philosophy. Meanwhile banks would make student loan decisions for poor students based on the likelihood of that education paying off in terms of a real job. The system would discourage poor students from choosing dead end majors.

Topic 28: Didn't free markets and inequality cause the economic

collapse in 2008?

The government intervention in the markets to subsidize housing caused the massive recession we saw in 2008. Everybody knows that the root of the crash was the mortgage crisis. But what most people don't know, as they couldn't care less about the boring realm of finance, is how the mortgage market was set up and how it all went crashing down.

The usual explanation is, of course, the easiest one—blame a red herring. In this case, most people blamed the banks. The banks gave out loans that they knew people couldn't pay back. They overexposed (put too much capital in the mortgage market) themselves to securities related to bundled mortgages (*Traditional Residential Mortgage Backed Security* (**TRMBS**)). Then they covered their positions with credit default swaps to insure themselves against catastrophic losses. It is all absolutely true the banks did all of the above.

Anyone who has ever lent money to a friend or dealt with credit in any capacity should know that there is a lot missing from the usual explanation of what the banks did to blow up the economy. The first problem being, "Why would the banks lend out their own money to somebody who can't pay them back?" Would you make a loan to a stranger for $50, knowing he would tell you to, "get lost", when you returned to collect? The second problem with the statement is, "Why would anybody then go on to buy these securities that were backed by mortgages that had a good chance of default?" Obviously, something is missing here.

To understand how the crash was a deviation from the free market principles and are tied to the activities of our compassionate politicians, we have to understand two entities— Freddie Mac and Fannie Mae. Fannie Mae and Freddie Mac were established during the New Deal by one of America's most remembered Presidents, Franklin D. Roosevelt. These two organizations were established to make mortgages more widely available to the public by being the investment bank for mortgage banks. Now what do I mean by that? An investment bank is just a bank that provides financial services for businesses. They help finance operations by appraising assets and using those value metrics to securitize debt (forgive me for the boring jargons).

Fannie and Freddie acted as investment banks for other banks by securitizing their assets, which in this case is the mortgages those banks gave out to homeowners (the balance of loans that are made by banks are considered assets and a liability for the borrower). What does a mortgage securitization look like, you might ask? Well, it's basically when you buy all the loans from a bank, and you pull them together into a fixed income "looking" product (bond). You then use the monthly mortgage payments made by Jon P. American to pay the holder of the bond on a monthly, quarterly, semi-annually, or annual basis. The bank continues to service the debt, which means that the bank just collects the payments from the borrower, and it funnels the money to the person structuring the bond. The bond structurer then makes the payments to the holder of the security.

It's pretty clear why everybody plays their part in this whole operation and why it all looks great on the surface. The bank sells the mortgages to Fannie and Freddie because they get all the money they loaned out back on the mortgages they issued. Plus, a little bit of the future interest payments without having to wait for the homeowner to pay them back, Fannie and Freddie are buying and bundling the mortgages because they're Government Sponsored Entities (GSE's) tasked with expanding homeownership by providing liquidity to the banks (quick money to make loans). The buyer of the security is in on it because they want a bond with a "safe" and steady return that they are looking for. The situation sounds like a win-win for everybody on the surface.

Look at this model long enough, and you see the inherent

flaw in it. The banks don't care much about who they issue mortgages to, as the second they make a loan, Fannie and Freddie buys the mortgage. Therefore, people who can't pay a mortgage for longer than a couple of years still get approved by the banks. The banks don't face market consequences (i.e. never getting paid back) for issuing the mortgage. Fannie and Freddie don't care about losing money because they are backed by the massive resources of the taxpayer. The buyer of the security doesn't think twice about losing money from buying the debt instrument, as it's basically backed by the government (i.e. they're protected by the taxpayer's dollars). Thankfully, the politicians who created this system were smart enough to see this massive potential problem. They limited the kind of mortgages that Fannie and Freddie could buy, i.e. set loan standards so only people with good credit history/rating qualified.

Now what's the problem with creating a program that only helps people with good credit, you might ask? By doing so you're just creating a program to help the well-off Americans finance housing easier, as those with higher credit rating scores tend to be wealthier. Over time, the government program did what all government programs do—it expanded to cover more people. Fannie and Freddie ended up backing the mortgage payments of poorer borrowers and also buying and securitizing more risky loans. Couple that with the low interest rates set by the Federal Reserve, ever increasing tax incentives for individual home purchases, and you have the recipe for the housing bubble that tanked the economy.

If you take Fannie and Freddie out of the equation, a recession caused by massive mortgage defaults would have never happened. Why? People with bad credit would have never gotten loans in the first place. The banks would have had to put up their own money if a borrower defaulted on a loan. They would have declined those with bad credit history/rating and a low down payment to put down on a house. The reason the argument that the banks messed up and blew up the economy is a common one is because it's a simple slogan that anybody can repeat. The above explanation is multifaceted and requires a good deal of knowledge

on how the financial system works to understand it.

Conclusion

It is my hope that this book has highlighted the point that simply wanting to help the poor is not enough. *The well intentioned economic policies that have been put in place to help the poor have wreaked havoc on the people, as it robs them of skills, prevents them from saving money to better themselves, and enables them to waste their own time and money to pursue counterproductive activities.* The programs and policies mentioned in this book should always be argued based on their effectiveness to alleviate the poor out of poverty and not their apparent merits.

The politicians and public should never make the mistake of thinking that their compassion and goodwill can defeat the laws governing economics and logic. I presented the cause and effect logic that economists have long talked about when presenting their arguments:

- If you make something more expensive, people will buy less of it. Therefore, raising the minimum wage will always cause unemployment among minimum wage workers. In the long run, this stunts their ability to acquire skills.

- If somebody receives more in benefits by performing Activity A than Activity B, then they will always choose to perform Activity A. Therefore, as welfare, in most cases, pays more through government benefits than a low-skilled worker would receive by working, they will always choose the government money over the low-paying job. This in turn robs people of opportunities to develop skills.

- If you subsidize people to engage in risky behaviors by lowering the costs of failure, they'll be more likely to engage in risky behavior. Therefore, if you subsidize the costs of higher education, a person who is not prepared to study a major with a future will likely waste precious time and money to go to college to get degrees with little or no practical application. According to the same rationality, if you insure banks from the risk of losing money on mortgage loans, they will give out loans to borrowers with poor credit history and those who have a high chance of defaulting on their mortgage payments.

There are no easy answers to the question of how we can lift people out of poverty. This is why Economics is known as "*The Dismal Science*". We have no easy answers, and most of our findings appear on the surface to be cruel. The conclusion most economists have come up with to alleviate poverty is to allow individuals to be free to make their own choices regarding the wages they are willing to work for, to not disincentive work with short-term monetary benefits that lead to long-term traps, and to not subsidize their failure so that they actively thinking about the consequences their choices have on their own futures.

The smartest message an economist can deliver to their friends and family on the topic of economics is silence. Any rational conversation about economics is going to end badly for them.

Appendix

1. "Characteristics of minimum wage workers, 2015: BLS Reports." U.S. Bureau of Labor Statistics. April 2016. Accessed August 29, 2016. https://www.bls.gov/opub/reports/minimum-wage/2015/home.htm.

2. "Labor Force Statistics from the Current Population Survey." U.S. Bureau of Labor Statistics. October 2015. Accessed August 29, 2016. https://www.bls.gov/opub/reports/minimum-wage/2015/home.htm.

3. Costco Wholesale Corporation (2015). 10-K Annual Report 2015. Accessed August 29, 2016, from SEC EDGAR website.

4. "QuickFacts." U.S. Census Bureau QuickFacts selected: UNITED STATES. Accessed August 29, 2016. https://www.census.gov/quickfacts/fact/table/US/PST045216.

5. DeHaven, Tad. "Corporate Welfare in the Federal Budget." Cato Institute. July 25, 2012. Accessed August 29, 2016. https://www.cato.org/publications/policy-analysis/corporate-welfare-federal-budget.

6. "Policy Basics: Introduction to Medicaid." Center on Budget and Policy Priorities. August 16, 2016. Accessed August 29, 2016. https://www.cbpp.org/research/health/policy-basics-introduction-to-medicaid.

7. "The Conference Board Total Economy Database™." The Conference Board. May 2017. Accessed August 29, 2016. https://www.conference-board.org/data/economydatabase/index.cfm?id=27762.

8. EXXON MOBIL CORPORATION (2015). 10-K Annual Report 2015. Accessed August 29, 2016, from SEC EDGAR website.

9. "Median Household Income in the Past 12 Months (in 2015 inflation-adjusted dollars)". American Community Survey. United States Census Bureau. 2015. Archived from the original on 17 April 2016. Accessed August 29, 2016.

10. Employment Policies Institute. (2017). *Employment Policies Institute | Minimum Wage: Teen Unemployment.* [online] Available at: https://www.epionline.org/minimum-wage/minimum-wage-teen-unemployment/ [Accessed 21 Sep. 2017].

11. "Entry-Level Graphic Artist Salary." Entry Level Graphic Artist Salary. September 16, 2017. Accessed September 22, 2017. https://www.payscale.com/research/US/Job=Graphic_Artist/Hourly_Rate/ebe62ac2/Entry-Level.

12. "Entry-Level Software Engineer Salary." Entry Level Software Engineer Salary. September 20, 2017. Accessed September 22, 2017. https://www.payscale.com/research/US/Job=Software_Engineer/Salary/4fd947de/Entry-Level.

www.ingramcontent.com/pod-product-compliance
Lightning Source LLC
Chambersburg PA
CBHW022041190326
41520CB00008B/675